AF228539

CRYPTIDS

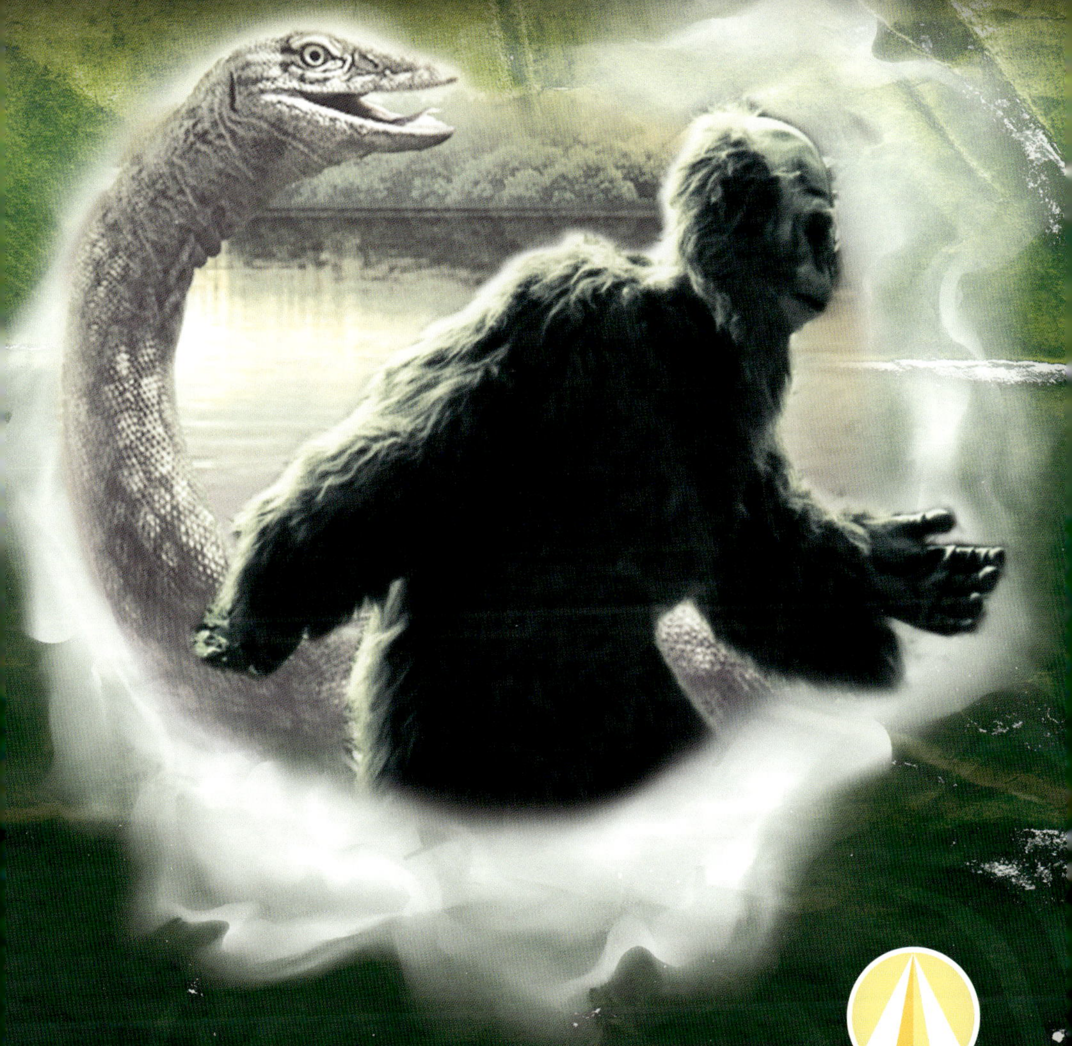

KENNY ABDO

Fly!
An Imprint of Abdo Zoom
abdobooks.com

abdobooks.com

Published by Abdo Zoom, a division of ABDO, P.O. Box 398166, Minneapolis, Minnesota 55439. Copyright © 2020 by Abdo Consulting Group, Inc. International copyrights reserved in all countries. No part of this book may be reproduced in any form without written permission from the publisher. Fly!™ is a trademark and logo of Abdo Zoom.

Printed in the United States of America, North Mankato, Minnesota.
102019
012020

Photo Credits: Alamy, iStock, Shutterstock
Production Contributors: Kenny Abdo, Jennie Forsberg, Grace Hansen
Design Contributors: Dorothy Toth, Neil Klinepier, Pakou Moua

Library of Congress Control Number: 2019941598

Publisher's Cataloging-in-Publication Data

Names: Abdo, Kenny, author.
Title: Cryptids / by Kenny Abdo
Description: Minneapolis, Minnesota : Abdo Zoom, 2020 | Series: Guidebooks to the unexplained | Includes online resources and index.
Identifiers: ISBN 9781532129346 (lib. bdg.) | ISBN 9781644942871 (pbk.) | ISBN 9781098220327 (ebook) | ISBN 9781098220815 (Read-to-Me ebook)
Subjects: LCSH: Cryptozoology--Juvenile literature. | Legendary animals--Juvenile literature. | Legends--Juvenile literature. | Pseudoscience--Juvenile literature. | Folklore--Juvenile literature.
Classification: DDC 001.944--dc23

Table of Contents

Cryptids 4

Classification. 8

Declassified. 12

In Media 20

Glossary 22

Online Resources 23

Index 24

CRYPTIDS

Whether hiding in the Himalayan mountains or being caught on blurry film deep within forests, cryptids have captured the curiosity of the world.

Owlman
of Mawnan
Chupacabra
Gambo
Dragon
Cynocephalus
Yeti
Mongolian
Death Worm
Sea Bishop
Orang-bati
Mbielu-mbielu-mbielu
Nessie
Kongamoto
Mothman
Troll
King Cheetah
Mermaid
Vampire
Grootslang
Cro
Creste
Phoenix
Giant Moa
Umibōzu
Thylacine
Hydra
Bungay Dog
6
P

Cryptids have been spotted all around the planet. Bigfoot stomps around America. Scotland is home to the Loch Ness Monster. And the Yeti has been seen throughout Asia.

CLASSIFICATION

The word cryptid is used to describe a figure that has been claimed to exist, but never proven to exist.

9

The term was created by **cryptozoologists**, who search for and study cryptids.

A cryptid can be classified in many ways. It can be a creature of myth and legend. Or a being that does not look like any known **species**. It can even be a **supernatural** or **paranormal** being.

DECLASSIFIED

Bigfoot, or Sasquatch, is a nine-foot-tall ape-like **hominid**. It roams the woodlands of the Pacific Northwest. But more recent sightings have been reported throughout America.

The Jersey Devil has been seen within the New Jersey Pineland forest. Its blood-curdling scream has haunted the state for more than 250 years. It has the body of a kangaroo and the head of a goat. It also has horns, a forked tail, and wings like a bat.

The Chupacabra wanders across South and Central America. It is the size of a small bear. It also has a row of spines from its neck to its tail. *Chupacabra* is Spanish for "goat-sucker." The name comes from its reputation for attacking **livestock**.

Yeti, or the Abominable Snowman, has been spotted in the Himalayan mountains. It gained notoriety in the 19th century when explorers found strange **tracks**. The tracks looked like they were made from a cross between a large wolf and a barefooted man.

The Loch Ness Monster, or Nessie, is one of the most famous cryptids. It lives in Scotland's largest lake, Loch Ness. Its deep waters have helped it avoid being seen or captured. Hugh Gray snapped the famous photo of Nessie in 1933.

Mothman was first spotted in Point Pleasant, West Virginia, in 1966. The red-eyed, winged creature has been a local legend ever since. Pictures of the Mothman were even captured in 2016!

Planted
and
Maintained
By The
Tu-Endie-Wei
Garden

"Legend of the Mothman"
On a chilly, fall night in November 1966, two young couples drove into the TNT area north of Point Pleasant, West Virginia, when they realized they were not alone.
What they saw that night has evolved into one of the great mysteries of all time; hence the Mothman Legacy began. It has grown into a phenomenon known all over the world by millions of curious people asking questions. What really happened? What did these people see? Has it been seen since?
It still sparks the world's curiosity - the mystery behind Point Pleasant, West Virginia's MOTHMAN.
Sculpture by
Artist and Sculptor
Bob Roach
New Haven, West Virginia

IN MEDIA

There have been several TV shows made based on hunting cryptids. Even so, no one has been able to provide **concrete** proof of their existence.

If you come across a cryptid, don't try to photograph or tame it. They are reportedly very dangerous. Cryptids, for now, will remain yeti'nother mystery to solve.

GLOSSARY

concrete – actually existing in physical form. Not theoretical.

cryptozoologist – a person who studies and tries to prove the existence of cryptids.

folklore – a story handed down from person to person.

hominid – a primate class that includes humans and some great apes.

livestock – a collection of farm animals.

paranormal – an occurrence beyond the scope of scientific understanding.

species – living things that are very much alike.

supernatural – a force beyond scientific understanding and the laws of nature.

track – a mark left by a person or animal in the ground.

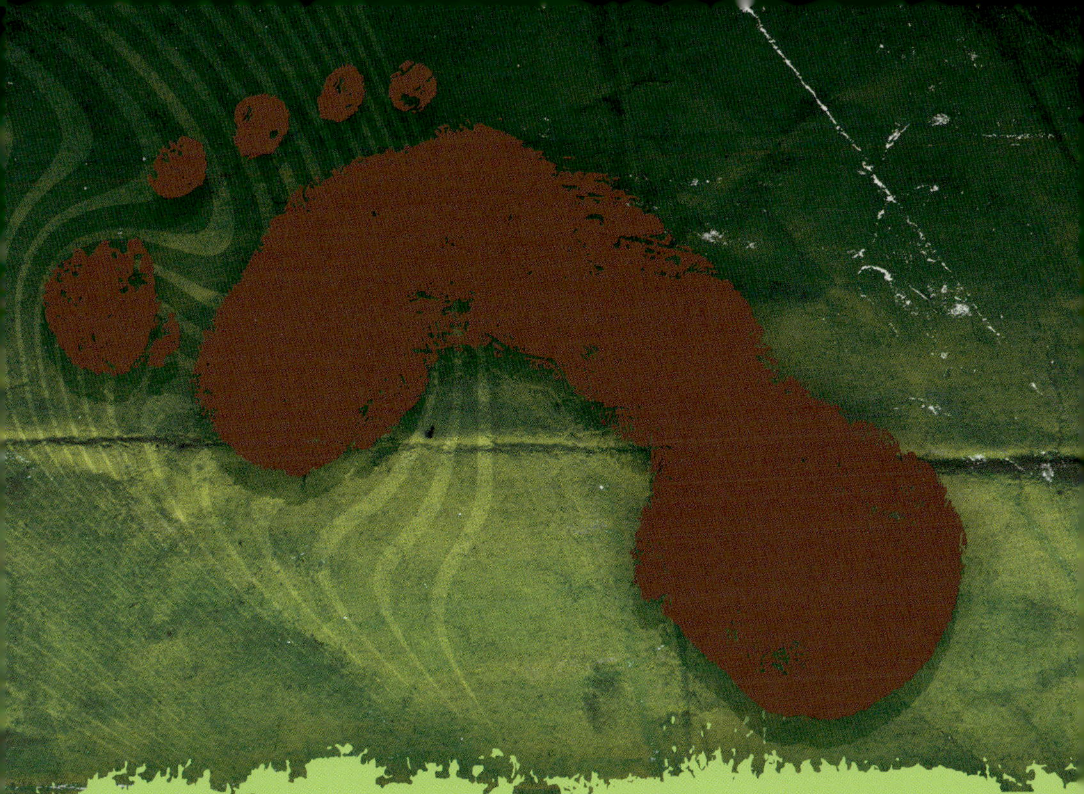

ONLINE RESOURCES

To learn more about cryptids, please visit **abdobooklinks.com** or scan this QR code. These links are routinely monitored and updated to provide the most current information available.

INDEX

Americas 7, 13, 15

Asia 7

Bigfoot 7, 13

Chupacabra, The 15

cryptozoologist 10

Gray, Hugh 17

Himalayan mountain range 4, 16

Jersey Devil, The 14

Loch Ness Monster 7, 17

Mothman 18

New Jersey 14

Scotland 7, 17

West Virginia 18

Yeti 7, 16, 21